READ it.

LOVE it,

LIVE it.

Congratulations
CHARLOTTE!

mr. & mrs. David Varley

BEFORE YOU BEGIN YOUR JOURNEY YOU MUST PROMISE YOURSELF TO PUT A MORATORIUM ON THE FOLLOWING STATEMENTS:

AS SOON AS I…
IF I…
ONCE I…
AFTER I…
WHEN I GROW UP I…
SOMEDAY I…

Right now, before we go any further, you must STOP scheduling procrastination and START practicing intention!

I woke up this morning. Someone else didn't.
I have another chance. Someone else doesn't.

FROM THIS MOMENT ON...
MAXIMIZE MY MOMENTS

There's a theory that says in the first 7 seconds that someone meets you they come to about 11 conclusions about you. These conclusions are based on how you're dressed, how you walk, how you talk, and what your body language is saying.

So basically, you have about 7 seconds to impact or influence how someone responds or reacts to your presence.

Think about that the next time you:

- Enter a classroom
- Pick up a job application from a restaurant, store, or movie theater
- Meet a friend, boyfriend, or girlfriend's parents
- Order food
- Go to a job interview
- Walk into a store
- Post something online
- Do a school or work presentation
- Perform stand up comedy

YOU'RE EITHER MAKING YOUR DREAMS COME TRUE OR SOMEONE ELSE'S

You have a dream inside you, maybe several that you're dying to see come true. Big dreams or small dreams, it doesn't matter. The question is, are you pursuing them? Every day of your life one of two things is happening; you are either working to make your dreams come true or you are a dream come true for someone else.

When your self-doubt causes you to skip a sport tryout or music or acting audition, you're a dream come true for those who want to eliminate the competition early.

When you sleep through or skip class, or drop out of school, you're a dream come true for those who profit from the rich staying rich and the poor staying poor, uneducated, and incarcerated.

When you believe your low self-worth means you deserve to be taken advantage of or abused in a relationship, you're a dream come true for those whose own poor self-esteem and insecurities manifest themselves in the way they treat others.

STOP BEING SOMEONE ELSE'S DREAM COME TRUE!

SPORTS, RHYME, OR CRIME IS NOT OUR ONLY HOPE

I love Hip Hop with all my heart, but there is some confusion about Hip Hop and rap music. As a side note, we don't even have to get into what mainstream media (i.e. favorite music video or radio stations) consider to be Hip Hop. The VAST majority of the time, what they label as being Hip Hop is actually the furthest thing from it. Hip Hop is a culture and lifestyle created with the intent to build and empower the urban community and those living in it. A LOT, not all, but A LOT of rap music promotes, celebrates, and glorifies the destruction of the urban community and those living in it. That's not Hip Hop.

So on that note, if you're a Black or Latino male, don't let rap music trick you into believing that being an athlete, a rapper, or a criminal are your only options. The rappers that promote this self-destructive mindset don't even believe that. Ask them if all they want to do is rap and most of them will say "Absolutely NOT." They understand the value of diversifying their interests.

And don't let them convince you that if this rap thing doesn't work out they will be back on the streets "hustlin'" in a heartbeat. That's a lie told to perpetuate a fake image they've created to establish so-called "street cred" amongst their fans. Most of your favorite gangsta rappers have never been real "gangstas", "pimps", or "hustlas" in the first place. If they were, it would be idiotic to confess your crimes to the world in a song.

So remember, just because they said it doesn't mean they did it, and even if they saw it, it doesn't mean they lived it. Don't let their fantasies dictate your reality.

Your Past
Does NOT Have to
DISQUALIFY
YOU
FROM YOUR
FUTURE

Your past does not have to disqualify you from your present or your future. Your destiny can begin to change right now. It starts with the choices you make from this moment on! Tell yourself, "I refuse to let the choices I made last year, last month, last week, yesterday or right before I opened this book disqualify me!"

The color of my skin does not disqualify me.
My ethnic heritage does not disqualify me.
The family I was born into does not disqualify me.
The neighborhood I live in does not disqualify me.
The school I go to does not disqualify me.
I will no longer let the grades I USED to get or the choices I USED to make (no matter how recent) disqualify me!
I AM NOT DISQUALIFIED!

I AM NOT DISQUALIFIED!

WHEN SOMEONE SAYS,

"YOU CAN'T"

WHAT THEY OFTEN MEAN IS,

"I CAN'T.

AND SINCE I CAN'T
I WOULD HATE IT IF YOU COULD."

DON'T LET OTHER PEOPLE'S
"CAN'T DO'S"
LIMIT YOUR
CAN DO'S OR
WILL DO'S.

APRENDA ESPAÑOL

En casi todas las otras naciones industrializadas, los alumnos pueden hablar dos, tres, o incluso a veces cuatro idiomas diferentes. Esto les da una ventaja enorme en el mercado global! Yo sé más que probable que usted y la mayoría de sus amigos no les gusta aprender un lenguaje o idioma extranjero, pero yo les estoy pidiendo que encuentren de alguna manera la determinación de aprender una segunda lengua una de sus principales prioridades.

Te prometo que si usted puede aprender español, chino, japonés, árabe, francés, alemán, lenguaje de señas o cualquier otro idioma, además de su lengua materna - que nunca sea desempleado y va a ser más difícil para las personas guardar secretos de usted!

LEARN SPANISH

صعود وتألق ©

The 3 most important languages to know after English are Mandarin Chinese, Arabic, and Spanish.

If you are in school taking a foreign language, make it your mission to LEARN the language, not just to pass the class. If you pass the class it's not guaranteed that you'll learn the language, but if you learn the language you're almost sure to pass the class.

BELIEVE IT OR NOT!

If you REALLY believe you can accomplish your dreams…

If you REALLY believe you can go to college…

If you REALLY believe you can start your own business…

If you REALLY believe you can change your eating and exercise habits…

If you REALLY believe you can work in professional sports…

If you REALLY believe you can make the Honor Roll at school…

If you REALLY believe you can be successful in the entertainment industry…

If you REALLY believe you can make a positive difference in your home, school, community, country, or the world…

If you REALLY believe you can start a new life, in a new city, a new state, or a new country…

If you REALLY believe, then how is that belief reflected in your attitudes, actions, and reactions? Don't just talk about it, be about it!

NOTE TO SELF...

Be as specific as possible.

- I believe I can...

- I believe I will...

- This is reflected in my actions because I...

- This is reflected in my RE-actions because I...

- This is reflected in my attitude because I...

I'D RATHER LOSE BECAUSE SOMEONE ELSE WAS BETTER THAN LOSE BECAUSE SOMEONE ELSE TRIED HARDER.

OPPOSITION PUTS YOU IN POSITION TO GLISTEN

Why do athletes like Lebron James, Adrian Peterson, David Beckham, or Serena and Venus Williams shine? One reason is because they are able to score against tremendous opposition. How impressive would Lebron be if every time he got the ball the defense stopped moving and just let him score at will? No one would be the least bit impressed with his skill because he didn't prove anything. What's more is he wouldn't be anywhere close to being the stellar athlete that he is because his skills would have never been put to the test. The same goes for each of these athletes and the same goes for you.

If you have people or circumstances in your life that are trying to hold you back or keep you down, just look at them as the defense trying to keep you from scoring. Don't run, dodge, or back down from their defense. Use it to make you better at offense. When you finally reach that goal or make that shot in life, your victory will be all the more impressive!

IMAGINE THAT!

Your imagination helps you to see pictures that have never been painted, create computer programs that have never been created, write screenplays that have never been written, tell stories that have never been told, solve problems with no apparent solutions, start businesses that have never been started, and think of ideas that make others say, **"Why didn't I think of that?"**

PEOPLE WITH INCREDIBLE IMAGINATIONS BECOME THE BEST:

Artists, film makers, investors, inventors, entrepreneurs, lawyers, writers, doctors, engineers, athletes, architects, computer programmers, chefs, marketing execs, interior decorators, fashion designers, storytellers, singers, composers, rappers, scientists, skateboarders, scholars and the list goes on and on…..

Your imagination helps you see things others can't see…yet. And in most areas of life, whether it's on the job, in school, or at an Easter-egg hunt, if you're the first to see something you end up winning!

HOW TO EXERCISE YOUR IMAGINATION:

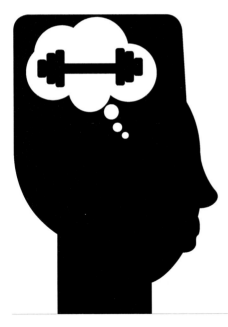

1. Read a novel

2. Write a one-page story

3. Draw a picture

4. Watch a movie with your eyes closed

5. Play with toys, play dough, or LEGOs

6. Take an acting class

7. Join an improv group

8. Color in a coloring book

9. Finger paint

10. Turn the volume down on a TV show and create your own dialog

---

This information and these simple exercises can truly help you become better at what you do or better at what you will become. The key is to be **INTENTIONAL** about exercising that part of your brain. The people in this world that know this and use their imaginations have a **HUGE** advantage over the people who don't. Start using your imagination today!

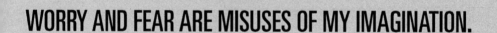

WORRY AND FEAR ARE MISUSES OF MY IMAGINATION.

FOCUS ON THE
PRO—Sequences

A lot of people will try to DIS-courage you from making bad choices by reminding you of all the consequences of those choices.

I know that doesn't work because it's hard for you to fathom anything bad ever happening as a result of your choices. One thing I will say is that the people who said, "It'll never happen to me," are the ones that "IT" happened to. You just don't know, so it probably isn't worth the risk.

But instead of focusing on the CON-sequences of your actions, I want to EN-courage you to meditate on what I call the PRO-sequences. What are the GOOD things that can happen to you and for you as a result of making GOOD choices as opposed to simply avoiding bad ones?

Right now stop, pick an area in your life where you want to see a good outcome, and write down some of the good choices you can make to ensure good PRO-sequences.

Be as specific as possible

Pick an area in your life that is important to you (i.e. Family, Faith, Academics, Athletics, Music, Art, Sports, College, Career, Important Cause, etc.)

PRO
SEQUENCES

Repeat this exercise as often as necessary for as many areas of your life as necessary.

Write a couple sentences about why this is important to you:

_____

_____

_____

_____

Make a list of positive choices you should make (not negative choices you should avoid) that will enhance this area of your life:

_____   _____

_____   _____

_____   _____

_____   _____

_____   _____

Make a list of PRO-sequences (positive results) of those positive choices:

_____   _____

_____   _____

_____   _____

_____   _____

_____   _____

When someone else's opinion of you means more to you than your opinion of yourself, you can become a slave to that person.

OPINIONS

I was really popular in high school, but I know that I sacrificed, compromised, and nearly killed myself (literally) trying to get popular and stay popular.

AND

We put so much stock into what other people think about us that if we're not careful we lose touch with our true self in the process.

The crazy thing is that the day after I (barely) graduated, I hardly saw any of those people in high school ever again. So the question I had to ask myself is, was it really worth it? The obvious answer is no.

ELBOWS

So think about it...who are you a slave to? Your boyfriend? Your girlfriend? The guys you hang with? The girls you spend time with? The cool clique you're trying to impress?

Opinions are like elbows, most people have at least one. So whose opinions of YOU are you making a priority? And are they really worth it? Don't be a slave to other people's opinions.

OTHER PEOPLE'S OPINIONS OF ME ARE THEIR FANTASY...NOT MY REALITY.

THERE ARE 3 KINDS OF PEOPLE WHOSE OPINIONS MATTER... PEOPLE WHO ARE **PUSHING** YOU FORWARD, PEOPLE WHO ARE **PROVIDING** YOU OPPORTUNITIES, OR PEOPLE WHO CAN **PAY** YOU MONEY.

PEOPLE WHO DON'T KNOW WHO THEY ARE
OFTEN ACT LIKE WHO THEY ARE NOT.

NOTE TO SELF...

Be as specific as possible.

I define myself as...

_____

_____

_____

_____

_____

_____

_____

_____

_____

_____

_____

_____

_____

_____

_____

_____

_____

_____

_____

_____

IF YOU DON'T DEFINE YOURSELF SOMEONE ELSE WILL.

Every word I say...

Every thought I create...

Every action I take...

Every reaction I have...

Every attitude I embrace...

Every pleasure I indulge...

MUST upgrade my life and the lives of others.

Every choice you make will either create chances and opportunities for you or take chances and opportunities from you.

CHOOSE WISELY!

FROM THIS MOMENT ON...
THERE ARE NO IMPOTENT CHOICES.

WITHOUT EVEN THINKING

Most of the time when you can start a story by saying, "Without even thinking I...," chances are it's going to end badly.

The power to think and choose is like a muscle, the more you exercise it, the stronger it becomes. It starts with understanding the difference between doing things impulsively and doing things instinctively.

Impulse means: Incitement to some un-premeditated action usually other than rational.

Instinct means: Your natural or inherent capacity.

I believe we all have a natural, inherent capacity to make choices that will better our lives and the lives of those around us.

An important step in mastering positive action is to first master positive RE-actions. Someone once said that, "Life is 10% what happens to you and 90% how you respond to it."

Try to save your "without even thinking" stories for choking victims, children chasing balls into the street, and calling 911.

DO NOT LET THE WORDS, "IT'LL NEVER HAPPEN TO ME" **ENCOURAGE** YOU TO MAKE BAD DECISIONS OR **DISCOURAGE** YOU FROM MAKING GOOD ONES.

STOP LIVING DOWN TO PEOPLE'S LOW EXPECTATIONS

If you know someone has low expectations of you, prove them wrong!
Often when we catch a vibe from someone like a teacher, coach, principal, parent, police officer, or even a so-called friend that they have low expectations of us, our tendency is to live DOWN to their expectations. We get a bad attitude with them and then in an act of defiance, we shut down!

THAT'S GOTTA STOP TODAY!!!
START PROVING THEM WRONG.

Start proving me RIGHT! I have expectations that you can and should do exceedingly amazing things with your life!

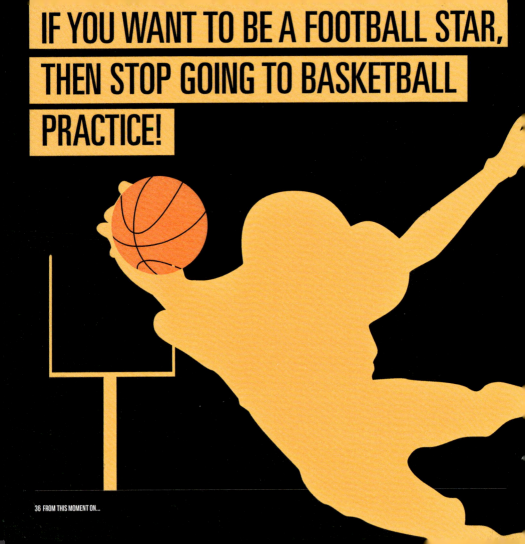

IF YOU WANT TO BE A FOOTBALL STAR, THEN STOP GOING TO BASKETBALL PRACTICE!

Let's say you want to be a football star, but all of your friends love basketball. They watch basketball, talk basketball, practice basketball, and play basketball all the time. It's obvious that if you want to excel in football, you're going to have to limit the time you spend with your basketball-loving friends and probably surround yourself with people on the same path and with the same passions as you. No hard feelings, it just is what it is.

The same goes for your life. If your desire is to pursue a lifestyle of excellence and success, you may have to change, limit, or even cut off some of the people you hang out with. Trust me, it's much easier to be pulled down by others than to pull others up.

FAKE IT TILL YOU MAKE IT???

If people put as much time and energy into making it as they do faking it, then making it might not be so difficult.

I am my most

RADIANT
ATTRACTIVE
DESIRABLE

self when I am operating in my *ELEMENT.*

I am operating in my *ELEMENT* when I am doing what I love,
when I am doing it well, and I am doing it for the right reasons.

FROM THIS MOMENT ON

STAY IN MY ELEMENT.

LOOKING beautiful and BEING beautiful are two different things.

If I spend MORE time doing it right, I'll spend LESS time doing it over.

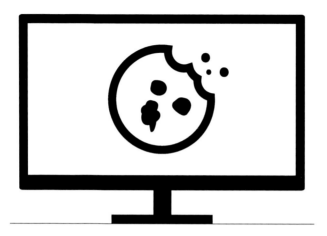

If I truly want MORE out of life, then I should buy LESS stuff, spend LESS time trying to impress others, watch LESS TV, and eat LESS junk food.

FROM THIS MOMENT ON...
LESS IS MORE

Unhappy people focus on everything they DON'T have.
Happy people focus on and are thankful for everything they DO have.

FROM THIS MOMENT ON
WAKE UP THANKFUL.
SPEND THE DAY HOPEFUL.
GO TO BED GRATEFUL.

If I quit I make it easier for those who haven't.

FROM THIS MOMENT ON...

NEVER GIVE UP

NOTE TO SELF:
WHAT IS YOUR CORE BELIEF?

Every successful company has a powerful mission statement. As individuals I believe it is close to impossible to experience personal success without a personal mission statement. Your core belief is that central truth that you stand on for your life. Malcolm X once said, "If you don't stand for something you will fall for anything." That is true, but I also think that if you don't believe in something, you will end up believing anything. That is why it's so important to establish your core belief. Maybe it's a famous quote or a verse of scripture from a religious text. It could be a family value or tradition. It could even be a line from a song or movie. The bottom line is you cannot step into success without standing on firm foundation. That foundation is your core belief.

For Example:

"My past doesn't disqualify me from my future." - Javier Sanchez

"Where there is no struggle, there is no strength." - Oprah Winfrey

"Be the change you wish to see in the world." - Gandhi

MY CORE BELIEF IS....

NOTE TO SELF:
WHO AND/OR WHAT DO I LIVE FOR?

Everyone is always talking about what they would DIE for. I want you to identify who or what it is you LIVE for. A lot of times when we're given the opportunity to make a bad choice, our attitude or response is, "What do I have to lose?" By identifying who and/or what we live for we give ourselves a reason not only to avoid bad choices, but also be intentional about making good choices. Knowing who and/or what you live for gives you a sense of purpose. Having a sense of purpose helps you discipline yourself. And disciplining yourself leads to an attitude and lifestyle of excellence and an opportunity to experience life to the fullest in a healthy, safe, and positive way. So identify the people or things that you live for. Is it your art? Academics? Athletics? Family? Faith? Future? You might have one thing. You might have five. What's important is that you identify who and/or what it is you live for.

I LIVE FOR...

_____

_____

_____

_____

_____

_____

_____

_____

_____

_____

_____

_____

_____

NOTE TO SELF:
WHAT IS THE EVIDENCE?

Earlier you identified who and/or what you live for. Now the question is...where is the Evidence or what is the proof? If you were on trial and the goal was to prove that you truly lived for what you say you lived for, whoever was making the argument would look to three areas; physical evidence, documented evidence, and the testimony of others. That means that if you TRULY live for what you say you live for, it should be demonstrated in your daily activities (physical evidence), it should be demonstrated by what you post on social media (documented evidence), and you shouldn't have to talk about what you live for because other people are telling your story (testimony of others). The bottom line is the Evidence should speak for itself so you don't have to.

THE EVIDENCE OF WHAT I LIVE FOR IS...

_____

_____

_____

_____

_____

_____

_____

_____

_____

_____

_____

_____

NOTE TO SELF:
WHAT IS AMAZING ABOUT YOU?

American youth collectively spend an average of $120 BILLION dollars every year on food, fashion, health & beauty products, and entertainment. They are the most marketed to age group in the history of the world. Young people see more commercials in a day than anyone else. Radio, TV, Internet, Magazines, Billboards, etc. You can easily be exposed to anywhere between 500 to 5,000 ads in just one day. Advertisers and marketers usually have two goals...to make you think something is wrong with you and to make you think that they care enough to fix you. Something is wrong with the way you look, the way you dress, what you're eating, or where you're going. Something is wrong with you because you're not buying this music or going to see this movie. You are "broke" and they can "fix" you. All you have to do is buy their stuff. Young people are sold that lie 500 to 5,000 times a day. That means that's 500 to 5,000 times a day we get told we're not cute or handsome enough, not cool enough, not strong enough, or not liked enough. We can see with young people experiencing high levels of depression, self-abuse, anxiety, and fear that there's a chance these ads could be working. Annual spending of $120 Billion dollars makes a pretty strong case for it. We MUST counter the 500 to 5,000 times a day we're told something is wrong with us by telling ourselves what is RIGHT with us. When we focus on the negative we are magnifying it and when you magnify something you are taking something small and making it appear bigger. What we need to do is amplify the positive things about ourselves. When you amplify something you are taking something strong and making it stronger. Take some time and be VERY INTENTIONAL about identifying all the amazing things about yourself. Then read those things aloud to yourself everyday.

THE AMAZING THINGS ABOUT ME ARE...

Example:
*I am
hardworking
I am intelligent
I am valuable
I am worthy
I am loveable
I am focused
I am creative*

_____
_____
_____
_____
_____
_____
_____
_____
_____
_____
_____
_____
_____

NOTE TO SELF:
WHAT DO I WANT TO BE REMEMBERED FOR?

Most of the time when we think about this question we are thinking about it in the context of after we die. One of the keys to massive success is to have this question in the forefront of our minds everyday. When you wake up in the morning you should ask yourself what you want to be remembered for at the end of the day. When you go into a classroom you should ask yourself what you want to be remembered for at the end of the class. When you go to a job interview, when you go on a date, when you do a school presentation, when you're given a project at work, when you perform on a stage, when you play in a sports competition, and when you are posting on social media, one of the most important questions you can ask yourself is...how do I want to be remembered? Think about it...if the last thing you said to someone was the last thing you could ever say to them...is that what you want to be remembered for? If the last thing you did to someone was the last thing you could ever do to them...is that what you want to be remembered for? If the last thing you posted on social media was the last thing you could ever post...is that what you want to be remembered for? Understand that LAST impressions are just as important as first ones.

I WANT TO BE REMEMBERED FOR...

FROM THIS MOMENT ON
I AM BECOMING...

Has anyone ever asked you, "What do you want to be when you grow up?" That question is misleading because it makes you think that you cannot BE or DO anything important with your life until you "grow up." The other problem is we only equate that question with a job or profession. Our identity should go way beyond what we do to earn an income. The way to reframe the question is to ask ourselves, "Who and what are we becoming RIGHT NOW?" Who and what are we becoming RIGHT NOW when it comes to our attitudes, our actions, and our aspirations?

I AM BECOMING…

I AM BECOMING MORE (ATTITUDE: I.E., POSITIVE, PEACEFUL, KIND, FOCUSED)

_____

_____

_____

I AM BECOMING BETTER AT (ACTIONS: I.E., STUDYING, EATING HEALTHY, HELPING OTHERS)

_____

_____

_____

I AM ASPIRING TO BECOME A/AN (DREAM JOB: I.E., ENTREPRENEUR, ENGINEER, PROFESSOR, PILOT)

_____

_____

_____

The aftermath of me is...

BETTER HAPPIER
CREATIVE **CLEANER**
EDUCATED PASSIONAT
LOVING SUCCESSFUL
STRONGER
ARTISTIC
INTENTIONAL
SMARTER
BLESSED

THE AFTERMATH OF YOU

Imagine what a better place this world would be if we made it our intention to leave all the people, places, and things we come in contact with on a daily basis better than how we found them.

Whether you known someone for 5 years or 5 minutes, make it your goal to leave them better than how you found them.

Whether you're settling in or just passing through, leave that place better than how you found it.

Whether you're buying it or borrowing it, leave that thing better than how you found it.

When you leave this earth, let people say that you left this world better than how you found it.

SHUT UP AND CREATE.™

SHUT UP AND CREATE! Yes, it sounds brash, but we're not really telling you to SHUT UP. What do we do when we are scared? We SCREAM and YELL for help. It's pretty much a natural reaction. The biggest obstacle in our own way is usually ourselves. We stop our own success by talking ourselves out of being great (screaming for help). I am guilty of this myself. I paid lip service to a lot of good ideas, but never put them to action because I was scared of being great.

Here are some examples of what I call *Scared-to-be-great Syndrome*:

- I have a great idea for a painting, I just don't have time to do it.
- I gotta finish the business plan before I launch.
- I am not creative enough!
- I don't have enough money.
- It's not the right time.
- They're better than me.

These are all things I have said to myself until I decided it had to change. A few years ago, I realized I wasn't reaching my dreams; I was just talking about my dreams. I realized that my heroes and mentors weren't on social media all day talking about what their dreams were. They were making them happen. So, I decided to make a change in my life. I just started doing, and it changed my life forever. I decided to silence my fear with action. Now I can say I am closer to my dreams and now if you hear me yelling it's about what I have been able to acomplish.

Here is what "Shut Up and Create" sounds like:

- I have had two solo gallery shows in the last year!
- My app is ranked top 50 in the app store!
- I just hired my first employee!
- That idea didn't work but now I can move on to the next one!
- I have made more money than I could have imagined
- The right time Is NOW!
- What work can we get done instead of having a meeting?

Having a plan is great. Plans give us structure and order. However, some of the greatest inventions, artwork, designs, and movements didn't come from plans. They came from someone or a group of people that decided they would SHUT UP AND CREATE.

- Marshall peace x love x create

Javier Sanchez

Javier loves helping people add process to their passion. As an author, performer, and filmmaker, Javier has the opportunity to deliver life-building messages to youth and adults all over the planet while keeping them entertained through comedy, spoken word poetry, and powerful stories from his own life. He absolutely loves his work, but the best part of what he does is coming home to his beautiful family!

experiencejavier.com

Marshall L. Shorts

Marshall L. Shorts, Jr. is a passionate creative that loves to help people reach their potential. As an artist, and a brand and visual communication consultant he has worked with artists, businesses, and arts organizations to help bring their visoins to reality. His passion for design is rivaled by his commitment to being a father, community resource and advocate. This has led him to starting a number of ventures aimed at exposing underserved communities to the arts and design. The Cleveland native and father earned his Bachelor of Fine Arts degree in Industrial Design with a minor in Advertising and Graphic Design from the Columbus College of Art & Design (CCAD). He is a member of Alpha Phi Alpha Fraternity, Inc.

soulotheory.com